Contents

Vanishing Wild

India is bursting with incredible creatures – frogs that dance, dolphins that "see" with sound, birds that boom and turtles that clean coral reefs. But many are now in serious danger. Their homes are shrinking, rivers are dirty and poaching is still a big problem. Some animals have fewer than 100 of them left in the wild. Can we protect them before they disappear forever?

Indian skimmers like to flock along riverbeds and estuaries

Why Are These Animals in Trouble?

Imagine losing your home, food and safety all at once. That's what's happening to these endangered animals. Forests are being cut for roads and buildings. Rivers are blocked by dams or are full of garbage. Some creatures are even hunted or stolen. With their homes disappearing, it's tough to survive. These animals aren't weak – they're just running out of space, food and clean air or water.

What Makes Them So Special?

These animals are amazing! The purple frog lives underground almost all year. Gharials have super skinny snouts built for fish-catching. Hawksbill turtles wear jewel-like shells and help keep coral reefs healthy by munching on sponges. And dancing frogs wave their legs to impress a mate! Many of these species live only in India and nowhere else on Earth. If we lose them, we lose something truly magical.

Can We Still Save Them?

Totally! Scientists, rangers and even schoolkids are helping. They clean rivers, protect nests, stop illegal hunting and plant more trees. Safe zones, breeding centres and eco-bridges are giving animals a better shot at life. You can help, too – by using less plastic, learning more and sharing their stories. Small actions can make a big difference. Every saved frog, turtle or dolphin is a big win for nature.

Superb large fan-throated lizards, found in dry grasslands

What If They Disappear Forever?

If these animals vanish, we lose more than just cool creatures. Forests may change. Rivers may grow dirty. Some plants won't grow without seed-spreading bats or poop-dropping monkeys! Nature works like a big team and every player matters. Saving animals isn't just about them, it includes us, too. When we start to protect them, we will also keep the planet healthy for everyone. No wild = no balance!

The hawksbill turtle can be seen in the coral reefs off Andaman

Great Indian Bustard

Find Me Here!

In Rajasthan's dry grasslands, especially in the Desert National Park. Look for tall birds walking through golden fields.

CRITTER STATS

Scientific name: *Ardeotis nigriceps*

Size: 1.2 m tall – like a 7- or 8-year-old child!

Weight: up to 10–15 kg

Lifespan: 12–15 years

Habitat: dry and open grasslands

Conservation status: critically endangered

Boom! A loud call echoes over the dry grasslands of north-western India carrying as far as half a kilometre – it's the great Indian bustard, India's heaviest flying bird! This grand bird once strode across grasslands in 11 Indian states, but is now mostly found only in Rajasthan.

When it's time to find a mate, this bird puts on quite the show! The male puffs up a special organ called the gular pouch – that's where the sound comes from – so it hangs like a showy balloon from its neck.

Males parade up and down in special display sites called leks – females are always welcome at the lek, but another male is quickly chased off!

Snack attack! These birds pick up bugs, seeds and even tiny reptiles while they walk. No fast food here – just fast pecks!

Bustards usually lay just one egg at a time, and only once during the year. At a time when their numbers are falling, every baby is precious!

The biggest threat to these birds are power lines connecting windmills in the desert. Bustards can't see straight ahead and fly into thick wires buzzing with electric power – and that usually spells death for the bird.

DID YOU KNOW?

The great Indian bustard almost became India's national bird but lost out to the peacock.

Scientists are now helping bustards lay eggs and raise young in enclosures, but what's equally important is saving their grassland habitat and not allowing it to be taken over for other activities.

Less than 150 of these magnificent birds are left in the wild. Yep, just a few birdy superheroes remain!

Gharial

Find Me Here!

On the Chambal river – look out for them in the water or on the sandbanks where they bask in sunny spots.

CRITTER STATS

Scientific name: *Gavialis gangeticus*

Size: up to 6 m – the length of 3 bicycles!

Weight: 150–250 kg

Lifespan: 40–60 years

Habitat: deep and fast-flowing rivers

Conservation status: critically endangered

Swoosh! A long snout slices through the water like a knife. Meet the gharial – a fish-eating crocodile with a toothpick snout! With its toothy grin and sleek body, this river reptile is an expert fisherman. But this ancient crocodile is in big trouble.

Gharials have super skinny snouts full of sharp teeth and strong neck muscles – just right for snapping up slippery fish in the water. Their jaws move fast, like lightning under the river! They are a little more clumsy on land, thanks to weak legs.

Gharial dads are hard-working! They guard eggs and later keep a close watch on baby gharials, using their long snouts to gently guide the little ones back to safety if they wander too far.

Gharials only eat fish, though young gharials may also snap up eat small fish, frogs, tadpoles and even insects.

Their favourite hangouts are clean, deep and fast-flowing rivers – that's tough to find when rivers are so polluted. And the many dams that slow down their flow don't help.

Breeding centres – where gharial eggs are carefully hatched under the care of scientists – and river clean-ups are helping gharials make a comeback.

DID YOU KNOW?

Male gharials have a pot-shaped bump on their snout called a "ghara" and hence their name. It helps them blow bubbles and make buzzing sounds to impress female gharials – like a fancy nose trumpet!

Gharials have over 100 teeth – more than any other crocodile cousin! Their super sharp teeth help them grab slippery fish fast, making them expert hunters in the water.

Gharials are ancient! They've been around since the time of dinosaurs and have swum through south Asia's rivers for millions of years, long before people showed up.

White-Bellied Heron

Find Me Here!

The heron can be found along the banks of the Noa-Dihing river that flows through Arunachal Pradesh's Namdapha National Park.

CRITTER STATS

Scientific name: *Ardea insignis*

Size: 1.3 m tall – like a 10- to 11-year-old kid!

Weight: 2–3 kg

Lifespan: 15–20 years

Habitat: foothills, rivers and forests

Conservation status: critically endangered

This is one bird that is hard to see. Not just because it's hard to spot – it can merge into the landscape despite its size – but also because so few of them remain in the wild. A tall and extremely shy creature, the heron is one of the rarest birds in the world.

This heron is a pillar of patience! It stands silently in the water, perfectly still, waiting for fish to swim close. With one fast jab of its beak, the meal is caught!

A solo player, this bird usually moves around on its own.

This is one silent operator. In the breeding season, when birds pair up to find mates, the heron can be heard calling in the early morning but it is largely silent during the day.

This bird is allergic to humans! At the first sound of people, this bird will take off to find a spot further along the river or in the forest close by.

Its home is disappearing. Dams, logging and road construction are ruining the rivers and trees it needs. Only about 50 are left in India!

DID YOU KNOW?

There are fewer than 250 white-bellied herons remaining in the wild.

Just a few birds pair up and nest each year – that's why their numbers are so small.

This bird is in danger of becoming extinct – and soon!

Indian Skimmer

Find Me Here!

Along clean stretches of rivers like the Chambal, Ganges and Mahanadi.

CRITTER STATS

Scientific name: *Rynchops albicollis*

Size: 40–43 cm – about the size of a crow

Weight: 250–300 g

Lifespan: 12–15 years

Habitat: riverbanks and estuaries

Conservation status: endangered

Zoom! A flash of black, white and orange streaks across the river's surface – it's the Indian skimmer! Fewer than 3,000 survive today, making this an endangered species.

The Indian skimmer's bottom beak is longer than the top one! It skims across the surface of water and uses its beak to scoop up tiny, slippery fish mid-flight.

When the lower beak comes into contact with prey, the upper beak snaps shut (with the fish trapped inside) and the meal is done.

Indian skimmers glide in tight, twisty flocks, zipping over the water in a streak of brilliant colours. It's a dazzling show right over the water!

Skimmers lay their eggs right on sandy riverbanks. But floods and human movement can crush these nests, making it tough for baby skimmers to hatch and grow up.

Skimmers are in trouble because dams, sand mining and dirty rivers are ruining their feeding spots and nesting places. They need clean, flowing rivers and safe sandbanks to survive and raise their chicks.

DID YOU KNOW?

Only three types of skimmers exist in the whole world! That makes every sighting of this bird really special.

These birds don't dive but instead catch fish close to the water's surface.

Male skimmers court female by performing a head-bobbing dance move and follow it up with a gift of fish.

Hawksbill Turtle

Find Me Here!

The islands of Lakshadweep, as well as reefs adjoining the Andaman and Nicobar Islands, are good places to spot them.

CRITTER STATS

Scientific name: *Eretmochelys imbricata*
Size: 60–90 cm shell length – like a folded umbrella
Weight: 45–70 kg
Lifespan: up to 50 years
Habitat: coral reefs and coastlines
Conservation status: critically endangered

Meet the coral reef sculptor in a shell suit! Gliding through coral castles, the hawksbill turtle is like a living jewel in the sea. Its beak-like mouth nibbles on sponges, keeping reefs clean. But beauty comes at a cost – its shell is so prized, it's nearly vanished from many coasts.

Hawksbill turtles keep the coral reefs healthy by eating sponges that smother the coral. Without them, reefs would struggle to survive. These little reef cleaners do a big job underwater!

Their shells shine with golden and amber patterns that look like stained glass. But this beauty makes them targets for illegal trade, even though it's banned across the globe.

During nesting time, females swim to the same beach where they were born. Even after crossing oceans, they always return home – guided by Earth's magnetic field that works like a natural GPS.

Under the cover of night, they dig soft nests and lay up to 150 eggs. Mama then returns to the sea and the eggs hatch after 60 days. Baby turtles must find their way to the ocean on their own.

It's not easy being a hawksbill. Plastic trash, fishing nets, beach construction and poaching all threaten them. Rising seas are also washing away their precious nesting spots.

DID YOU KNOW?

Baby hawksbills are only about 5 cm long when they hatch, but they grow fast – as they have to survive on their own from day one!

Hawksbills can stay underwater for 45 minutes without coming up for air – that's perfect for exploring reefs and looking for snacks.

Hawksbills are known to be "keystone species" because coral reefs can weaken or collapse without them. That's how important they are to ocean life!

Lion-Tailed Macaque

Find Me Here!

Spotted in the rainforests of the Western Ghats.

CRITTER STATS

Scientific name: *Macaca silenus*

Size: 40–60 cm (excluding tail) – like a small dog

Weight: 2–10 kg

Lifespan: 20 years

Habitat: tropical evergreen forests

Conservation status: endangered

High in the canopy of the Western Ghats swings a monkey with a lion-like tail and mane. This is a primate built for the treetops. But roads and farms are slicing its forest into pieces and if we don't act soon, the Western Ghats could lose one of its rarest mammals.

The lion-tailed macaques wander about in groups of 15 or more called a troop.

These monkeys talk a lot. They whoop, squeak, grunt, smack their lips and even make faces to communicate.

They love eating wild fruits (jackfruit is a favourite) but will also eat flowers and insects if fruits are scarce. They disperse the seeds of fruit they eat and help the forest grow.

As forests recede and roads split their habitats, macaques must descend to the ground – where cars and people pose threats.

To help these monkeys cross busy roads, canopy bridges have been built in a few places.

With more humans building homes in their forest habitat, macaques have sadly started raiding garbage dumps for unhealthy fast food.

DID YOU KNOW?

Their tails have fluffy tufts at the end that look like a feather duster, just like lions! Macaques use their tails for balance as they leap and climb through the forest canopy like acrobats.

In an undisturbed habitat, lion-tailed macaques will hardly ever descend to the ground. They are true tree-lovers, spending nearly their whole lives swinging, climbing and jumping through India's rainforest treetops.

These macaques are found only in the Western Ghats and nowhere else in the world!

Superb Large Fan-Throated Lizard

Find Me Here!

Dry grasslands and rocky plains of Maharashtra, Karnataka and the Deccan Plateau – especially in the summer heat.

CRITTER STATS

Scientific name: *Sarada superba*

Size: 8–12 cm (tail not included) – like a mouse!

Weight: up to 15 g

Lifespan: 4–5 years

Habitat: dry scrub and in cracks of plateau rocks

Conservation status: regionally threatened

In the sun-baked grasslands of India's west, a little lizard puts on a mighty show! The superb large fan-throated lizard isn't just colourful – it's a mini flag-waving champion. But it's not all fun and games – these lizards are deeply threatened by shrinking scrublands and we have to save their habitat to keep this gem around.

Male lizards don't need to shout – they have something far better to call attention to themselves! They flash a rainbow-coloured throat fan called a dewlap to impress females or warn rivals to back off.

These lizards love the heat! When the sun's blazing, they come out to play, zipping across rocks and striking cool poses like tiny yoga champs in the desert.

Warmth is everything for them. They need dry, open land to stay fast and alert. With quick moves and sharp eyes, they're expert insect catchers on the run.

Their world is shrinking. Roads, farms and grazing animals damage their homes, making it harder for them to survive and stay safe.

They were only discovered in 2016 – a brand-new addition to India's amazing list of lizards found nowhere else on Earth. What a cool surprise for science!

DID YOU KNOW?

The throat fan changes colour depending on the light – sometimes it flashes blue, orange, or even purple – like a living rainbow.

They do push-ups to show off to females or send a warning to rivals that "this is my space!"

When threatened, these lizards can run at remarkable speeds, comparable to that of rabbits, allowing them to swiftly escape predators.

Peacock Tarantula

Find Me Here!

Forest canopies of Andhra Pradesh – hiding inside tree hollows, bark crevices and dark nooks in tropical dry forests.

CRITTER STATS

Scientific name: *Poecilotheria metallica*

Size: leg span up to 20 cm – as big as a dinner plate!

Weight: 30–40 g

Lifespan: 10–12 years

Habitat: forest canopy and tree hollows

Conservation status: critically endangered

Some images in this chapter are not from India.

Shimmering like sapphire in the shadows, the peacock tarantula is one of the world's most colourful spiders. Found only in India, it's as rare as it is beautiful. But with forests fading and increasing pet trade, this stunning spider might vanish from the treetops before we truly know it.

Its body shines electric blue like a gemstone! The bright colours might scare off predators or help find mates – but mostly, they amaze people. It's one seriously colourful and cool spider!

It spins silky webs inside hollow trees but doesn't just wait around. It pounces on bugs using ambush attack – super fast and silently! This spider is a sneaky hunter with ninja moves.

Even though it looks scary, it's really shy and almost never bites. It hides most of the time and only comes out at night to catch dinner.

Collectors love its shiny colours, but that's a problem. People take them away from the wild and forests are being cut down too. No wonder it's in big trouble.

Scientists say it's one of the rarest tarantulas on Earth, found in just one tiny forest area! That's why protecting its home in Andhra Pradesh is super important for keeping this species alive as it is the only blue species of the genus! Exciting, right?

DID YOU KNOW?

Its blue colour isn't from pigment – it's a light trick! Tiny hair structures bend light to make that shimmering blue. No paint, no dye – just amazing spider science!

Fangs out, but don't freak out! Yes, it's venomous – but not dangerous to humans. Its has more bark than bite, and the bite comes in handy for scaring off would-be predators or nosy threats.

This spider's story is the comeback tale of the century! Scientists thought it was extinct for over 100 years... until they rediscovered it in 2001, chilling in a forest like it never left.

Kolar Leaf-Nosed Bat

Find Me Here!

Only one known cave in Hanumanahalli, Kolar district, Karnataka – inside granite boulder formations.

CRITTER STATS

Scientific name: *Hipposideros hypophyllus*

Size: about 6 cm – like your computer's space bar!

Weight: 10 g

Lifespan: 10–12 years

Habitat: rock caves and granite hills

Conservation status: critically endangered

Deep inside a single granite cave in Karnataka flutters a tiny, leaf-faced bat. The Kolar leaf-nosed bat is so rare, it might be India's most endangered mammal. With big ears and a nose shaped like a leaf, it hunts quietly at night – but its only home is under serious threat.

This tiny bat has a wacky leaf-shaped nose! It's not for decoration – it helps the bat send sound signals to fly safely through the dark. Nature's coolest built-in navigation system!

It hunts at night, using sound to track flying insects. It swoops, zips and gulps them mid-air – like a flying, bug-hungry vacuum cleaner!

This bat's only home is a hidden cave in Karnataka. But granite mining threatens the habitat. If the cave goes, this little bat could disappear forever.

Luckily, some scientists and locals have joined forces to save the species! They're guarding the cave, tracking bat numbers and working hard to stop mining.

Recent studies show that this bat eats mostly moths and beetles, making it a vital pest controller for nearby crops – so saving it helps farmers too!

DID YOU KNOW?

There are only about 100 of these bats left in the wild. That's fewer than the number of kids in a grade at most schools – each one is super special and important!

The bat's cave is now marked as protected, which helps. But sneaky illegal mining still happens nearby, putting these rare, echo-loving bats at serious risk.

It uses a "leaf-nose" sonar system! That funny-shaped nose helps the bat bounce sound off surfaces – like a living radar dish in the dark.

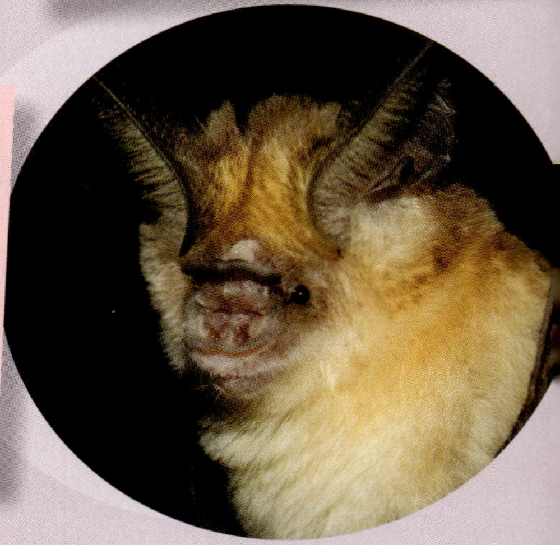

Bugun Liocichla

Find Me Here!

Eaglenest Wildlife Sanctuary in the Himalayas of eastern Arunachal Pradesh.

CRITTER STATS

Scientific name: *Liocichla bugunorum*
Size: about 22 cm – as big as a bulbul
Weight: around 40 g
Lifespan: unknown in wild
Habitat: montane forest undergrowth
Conservation status: critically endangered

In a misty forest, a bird with a flash of red and yellow in its wings flits past. Meet the Bugun liocichla – a rare bird found in just one forest patch in India. Its discovery is recent and was announced only in 2006. It is only the third new species of bird to be discovered in India after Independence.

It lives in just one small forest area in the Eaglenest Wildlife Sanctuary, making it one of the rarest birds in the world today.

The elusive bird is named after the Bugun tribe of Arunachal Pradesh, in whose forests it was first seen.

The tribe is extremely proud to have a species named after it. Today, hunting is banned in the forest that the Bugun liocichla calls home. Instead, that forest is part of the Singchung Bugun Village Community Reserve.

For a bird that looks so different from others, it went unnoticed for many years. Goes to show how few of them there possibly are.

When a new bird is discovered, a specimen of the species is usually collected for scientific research. But that wasn't done for the Bugun, since such a small population survives.

DID YOU KNOW?

The Bugun liocichla was discovered in 1996 by Ramana Athreya, an astronomer and ecologist from Pune.

It features on a stamp released by the department of posts in 2012.

This shy bird lives in the same forest all year round and does not migrate.

Spot Them Here!

Follow the pug marks to find some of the best places to spot India's amazing and rare wildlife!

Fact Finder

"Great Indian Bustard." *BirdLife International*, https://www.birdlife.org/datazone/speciesfactsheet.php?id=2644

"Great Indian Bustard." *Sanctuary Asia*, https://www.sanctuarynaturefoundation.org/species/great-indian-bustard

"Gharial." *IUCN Red List*, https://www.iucnredlist.org/species/8966/3148549

"Gharial." *Wildlife SOS*, https://wildlifesos.org/animals/gharial/

"White-bellied Heron." *BirdLife International*, https://www.birdlife.org/datazone/speciesfactsheet.php?id=3815

"White-bellied Heron." *Zoological Society of London (EDGE of Existence)*, https://www.edgeofexistence.org/species/white-bellied-heron/

"Indian Skimmer." *BirdLife International*, https://www.birdlife.org/datazone/speciesfactsheet.php?id=3094

"Indian Skimmer." *Roundglass Sustain*, https://roundglasssustain.com/photo-stories/indian-skimmer-bird

"Hawksbill Sea Turtle." *IUCN Red List*, https://www.iucnredlist.org/species/8005/12881238

"Hawksbill Turtle." *WWF India*, https://www.wwfindia.org/about_wwf/priority_species/marine_turtles/hawksbill_turtle/

"Lion-tailed Macaque." *IUCN Red List*, https://www.iucnredlist.org/species/12558/50140979

"Lion-Tailed Macaque." *NePrimate Conservancy*, https://neprimateconservancy.org/lion-tailed-macaque/

"Fan-throated Lizard." *Roundglass Sustain*, https://roundglasssustain.com/species/fan-throated-lizards-a-flash-of-fabulous

"Sitana ponticeriana." *IUCN Red List*, https://www.iucnredlist.org/species/172653/6901373

"Peacock Tarantula." *IUCN Red List*, https://www.iucnredlist.org/species/64884/12771691

"The Peacock Tarantula." *Critter Science*, https://critter.science/the-peacock-tarantula/

"Kolar Leaf-nosed Bat." *IUCN Red List*, https://www.iucnredlist.org/species/10147/3198495

"Kolar Leaf-nosed Bat." *Bat Conservation International*, https://www.batcon.org/our-work/species-directory/kolar-leaf-nosed-bat-hipposideros-hypophyllus/

"Bugun Liocichla." *BirdLife International*, https://www.birdlife.org/datazone/speciesfactsheet.php?id=32562

"Bugun Liocichla." *eBird*, https://ebird.org/species/buglio1

Credits

Writer: Ushashree M

Designer: Haitenlo Semy

Picture Credits

iStockphoto: cookelma, #1057558532; mihir_joshi, #2177311922; ePhotocorp, #2180732687; mihir_joshi, #2177312413; mihir_joshi, #2177312515; mihir_joshi, #2177312586; ePhotocorp, #2190334241; boryak, #104257773; RichLindie, #136144159; riskms, #175949673; DKart, #802769922; RichLindie, #1224746262; Wirestock, #1224746262; Wirestock,#1433343260; richcarey, #1252581912; Brooke Speakman, #2209834046; RainervonBrandis, #183793853; Fernando Frazao, #1224659458; cookelma, #535939461; richcarey, #1252581934; WhitcombeRD, #2191235088; mihir_joshi, #1404060751; ePhotocorp, #1420903703; ePhotocorp, #1459057333; mihir_joshi, #1404060542; mihir_joshi, #1404060713; mihir_joshi, #1403692619; CathyKeifer, #119582428; Wirestock, #1446621313; Renee OConnor, #1177464641; kaew6566, #1303452005; Kaan Sezer, #1182416455; GlassEyeStock, #1140118008; Suneet Bhardwaj, #1083036916; nkmswot, #1141474244; Liz Leyden, #469574684; ePhotocorp, #2190334257, Zocha_K, #2010552821; Zocha_K, #1263025199; PrinPrince, #658800060; BirdHunter591, #1251302267; sutiporn, #958771610; BirdHunter591, #1159122821; PrinPrince, #1019184510; Thamrongrat Tanomtham, #1160506658; jbhavya, #2188157981; Ranzi Photography, #2211565668; Sushil Bisht, #1326195938; ePhotocorp, #1286090764; Adisak Mitrprayoon, #1450620535; EyeEm Mobile GmbH, #2197720861; 49pauly, #1262297271; teptong, #880782552; Wirestock, #1447860875; Jayantibhai Movaliya, #2181786743; Aniful Izza, #1962474166; ePhotocorp, #1358187398; Jayantibhai Movaliya, #2162010322; pixbox77, #1056455412; ePhotocorp, #1464047592; Raghu_Ramaswamy, #1057171064; Anand RJ, #1411054333; ePhotocorp, #1004714804; ePhotocorp, #1263782289; Raghu_Ramaswamy, #1057170976.

Wikimedia Commons: Great Indian Bustard, Saurabh Sawant; Great Indian Bustard Ardeotis nigriceps by Dr. Raju Kasambe; Great Indian Bustard, Saurabh Sawant; gharial in Prague Zoo by Miroslav Bobek; A crocodilian Gharial mother and young by Goodfriend19; Gavialis gangeticus by Cliff; Gharial male by Nireekshit; Gharial (Gavialis gangeticus) female and juvenile by Charles J. Sharp; White-bellied Heron at Namdapha by Rajkimar99; White-bellied Heron Ardea insignis nest by Dr. Raju Kasambe; White-bellied heron in Namdapha Tiger Reserve by Rohit Naniwadekar; Eretmochelys imbricata by Kora27; Superb large fan-throated lizard Sarada superba by Krishna Khan; Picture of a juvenile female poecilotheria regalis by Morkelsker; Kolar Leaf nosed bat by Rajesh Puttaswamaiah; Kolar Leaf nosed bats by Rajesh Puttaswamaiah; Bugun Loichichla by Muk.Seh; Lion-tailed macaque canine by Kalyanvarma; Lion-tailed Macaque (Macaca silenus) in India by Kalyanvarma; Indian Skimmers Gliding over India's majestic rivers by Shiv's fotografia; Indian Skimmers by Shiv's fotografia; Indian skimmers over Chambal by Kandukuru Nagarjun; Indian Skimmers by by Shiv's fotografia; Indian Skimmer by Jayanth Sharma.

iNaturalist: White-bellied Heron (Ardea insignis) by Rohit Naniwadekar; Bugun Liocichla (Liocichla bugunorum) by James Eaton; Bugun Liocichla (Liocichla bugunorum) by James Eaton.

Unsplash: underwater photography of turtle by Derek Oyen.

Independent sources: White-bellied Heron in Namdapha pictures by Shashank Dalvi; Superb Large Fan-throated Lizard (Sarada superba) by Rohit Naniwadekar; Kolar Leaf Nosed Bat (Hipposideros hypophyllus) photos by Rajesh Puttaswamaiah; Lion-tailed Macaque, Valparai India photos by Shashank Dalvi; Lion-tailed macaque by N.A. Naseer; Bugun L by Adhirup Ghosh; Bugun Liocichla, Eaglenest pictures by Shashank Dalvi; Bugun Liocichla by
Mohit Mehta.

Map: Syailendra Gupta Muliawan, India Vectors by Vecteezy.

First published by Juggernaut Books 2025

10 9 8 7 6 5 4 3 2 1

P-ISBN: 9789353459345
E-ISBN: 9789353458775

Printed at Nutech Print Services - India